W9-AFD-000

Rookie Biographies®

Neil Armstrong

by Dana Meachen Rau

Content Consultant
Nanci R. Vargus, Ed.D.
Professor Emeritus, University of Indianapolis

Reading Consultant
Jeanne M. Clidas, Ph.D.
Reading Specialist

Children's Press®
An Imprint of Scholastic Inc.
New York Toronto London Auckland Sydney
Mexico City New Delhi Hong Kong
Danbury, Connecticut

Library of Congress Cataloging-in-Publication Data
Rau, Dana Meachen, 1971-.
  Neil Armstrong/by Dana Meachen Rau; content consultant, Nanci R. Vargus, Ed.D.
professor emeritus, University of Indianapolis; reading consultant, Jeanne Clidas,
Ph.D.
    pages cm. — (Rookie biographies)
  Includes index.
  ISBN 978-0-531-21063-5 (library binding) — ISBN 978-0-531-24984-0 (pbk.)
1. Armstrong, Neil, 1930-2012—Juvenile literature. 2. Astronauts—United States—
Biography—Juvenile literature. I. Title.

 TL789.85.A75R38 2014
 629.450092—dc23 [B]   2013034806

Produced by Spooky Cheetah Press
Poem by Jodie Shepherd
Design by Keith Plechaty

© 2014 by Scholastic Inc.

1 2 3 4 5 6 7 8 9 10 R 23 22 21 20 19 18 17 16 15 14

Photographs © 2014: Corbis Images/Bettmann: 4, 31 top; Defense Imagery/NASA/
Bill Ingalls: 27, 30 right; Landov/Mark Avino/NASM/Smithsonian Institution/Reuters:
28; NASA: 16 (Chris Cohen), cover, 15, 19, 20, 23, 24, 30 left, 31 center top, 31 center
bottom, 31 bottom; National Air and Space Museum, Smithsonian Institution: 3
top left, 3 top right, 3 bottom; Naval History and Heritage Command: 11; The Ohio
Historical Society: 8, 12.

Maps by XNR Productions, Inc.

Table of Contents

★ 4

Meet Neil Armstrong

Neil Armstrong always dreamed of being a pilot. In time, that dream would take him all the way into outer space. On July 20, 1969, Neil became the first person to walk on the moon. He explored farther than anyone ever had before.

This photo shows Neil in his space suit.

Neil Alden Armstrong was born on August 5, 1930. He grew up in Ohio with his parents; his sister, June; and his brother, David. Neil loved to read and learn. In his first year at school, he read more than 100 books! He was such a good student that he skipped second grade.

Neil was born in Wapakoneta, Ohio

MAP KEY

Ohio

● Town where
Neil Armstrong
was born

CANADA

Lake
Erie

NY

Michigan

PA

●Wapakoneta

Ohio

Indiana

West
Virginia

Kentucky

Virginia

8

This photo of Neil and his sister was taken when Neil was about five years old.

When he got a little older, Neil worked at a drugstore to earn money for flying lessons. He had to work for about 23 hours to earn enough money for each lesson! Neil got his pilot's license when he was only 16.

FAST FACT!

Neil learned how to fly a plane before he learned how to drive a car.

Flying High

Neil went to college to study the science of flying. He also learned about building engines and other machines. Neil chose to leave college to help the United States in the Korean War. He became a Navy fighter pilot and flew 78 **missions**.

This is a photo of Neil in his Navy flight suit.

After the war, Neil returned to school. He met Janet Shearon. They both finished college and then got married in 1956. In time, Neil and Janet had two sons and a daughter. Neil and Janet moved to California so Neil could work as a test pilot.

Neil is pictured with his wife and their two sons.

Neil's job was to test-fly X-15 rocket planes. He shared his ideas of how to make the planes even better. People noticed what a great pilot Neil had become. NASA wanted him to become an **astronaut** and fly in space.

FAST FACT!

NASA stands for the National Aeronautics and Space Administration. NASA is part of the U.S. government and is in charge of space exploration.

David Scott

Neil Armstrong

Gemini 8, Neil's first mission, took place in 1966. He and astronaut David Scott had to join their spacecraft with another ship while floating through space! Neil **docked** the two spacecraft successfully, but then they spun out of control. Neil's quick thinking saved the day. The astronauts returned safely to Earth.

FAST FACT!

When Neil was an astronaut, spacecraft "splashed down" into the ocean when they returned to Earth. They did not land on an airstrip like space shuttles.

Man on the Moon

Neil's next space mission would change the world forever. NASA wanted to send astronauts to the moon. Neil, Buzz Aldrin, and Michael Collins were chosen for the *Apollo 11* mission. The astronauts trained by practicing with the spacecraft, space suits, and other equipment.

In this photo, Neil practices collecting samples from the moon.

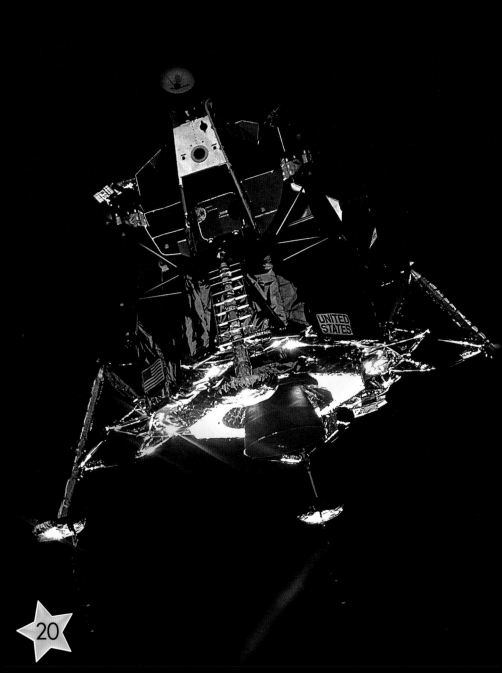

Apollo 11 launched on July 16, 1969. It took more than three days to get to the moon. Then the spacecraft split into two parts—*Columbia* and *Eagle*. Michael stayed in *Columbia*. Neil and Buzz took *Eagle* to the moon's surface. On the way down, the computer failed and the spacecraft almost ran out of fuel. Neil piloted *Eagle* to a safe landing on the moon.

This is a photo of *Eagle* taken from inside *Columbia*.

On July 20, Neil put on his bulky space suit and helmet. Then he became the first person to set foot on the moon. He said: "That's one small step for man, one giant leap for mankind." Neil and Buzz spent the next two hours doing **experiments** and collecting moon rocks.

FAST FACT!

Neil said the moon's surface was like powder. It stuck to his space suit and moon boots.

Neil and Buzz planted an American flag on the moon.

When the astronauts returned, they were kept in a trailer, separated from everyone else, for three weeks. NASA wanted to be sure they did not bring back unknown germs from the moon.

Back Home

After the astronauts rested, *Eagle* took off from the moon and docked with *Columbia*. The astronauts were ready to return to Earth. When they landed in the Pacific Ocean, the whole world celebrated their return.

Neil was famous after his moon landing. He worked at NASA for a while. Then he wanted a quieter life. Neil moved back to Ohio and bought a farm. He taught classes and worked in business. He sometimes gave speeches about the moon landing.

Neil enjoyed giving speeches, where he could share his love of flying with others.

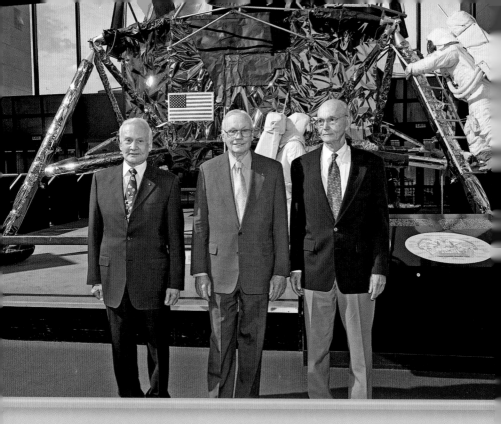

Timeline of Neil Armstrong's Life

1950–1952
flies planes in Korean War

1930
born on August 5

1962
joins the astronaut program

Buzz, Neil, and Michael pose in front of the lunar landing module at the Smithsonian National Air and Space Museum in Washington, D.C.

Neil Armstrong died on August 25, 2012. People will always remember him as the first explorer of an unknown place. His love of flying took him all the way to the moon.

1966
flies on *Gemini 8* mission

2012
dies on August 25

1969
lands on the moon

29

A Poem About Neil Armstrong

Neil always dreamed of being a flier—
both day and night, awake, asleep.
He first flew planes, then aimed much higher
and on the moon, took a giant leap!

You Can Be an Explorer

- Be adventurous! Do not be afraid to try something you have never done before.

- Learn as much as you can about people and places all around the world.

- Be curious! Ask questions and then search for the answers.

Glossary

astronaut (ass-truh-NAWT): someone who travels in space

docked (dokt): joined spacecraft in space

experiments (ek-SPER-uh-ments): scientific tests or activities to learn something new

missions (MISH-uhns): certain assignments or jobs

Index

Facts for Now

Visit this Scholastic Web site for more information on Neil Armstrong:
www.factsfornow.scholastic.com
Enter the keywords **Neil Armstrong**

About the Author

Dana Meachen Rau has written more than 325 books for children, including lots of nonfiction and early readers. She looks at the moon through her telescope with her husband and children in Burlington, Connecticut.